we were all afraid

joan cofrancesco

authorHOUSE®

AuthorHouse™
1663 Liberty Drive
Bloomington, IN 47403
www.authorhouse.com
Phone: 1 (800) 839-8640

Published by AuthorHouse 02/26/2016

ISBN: 978-1-5049-8268-9 (sc)
ISBN: 978-1-5049-8267-2 (e)

Print information available on the last page.

This book is printed on acid-free paper.

"The living owe it to those who no longer can speak to tell their story for them."
—Czslaw Milosz

syracuse
rome
utica
croton
poughkeepsie
this poem
is taking me
to you

on a train
from syracuse to nyc
my first love
my city lights pocket book
#19 *lunch poems*
in my leather jacket

december moon
pulling the train
through green norwegian firs
glistening with snow
to nyc

gershwin
the music
of the train
along the tracks

9/11

reading
the book of secrets
my black cat
beside me
looking into
the sky

watching the news
at a bar in downtown manhattan
drinking miller high life
a cloud
of smoke
rolls by

my cat stretches
and yawns
then stares at me
on the bed
reading lorca
we have nowhere to go

in the village
drinking coors lite
listening to patsy's
crazy
fingering a thin collection
of chinese poetry
a black cat rubs
against me

incense
rises
reading
crow
by
hughes

synergies among
pregnant women
ufo's
clocks
televisions
men with
dog heads
crawling babies
the world
trade center
as two
phalluses
keith
haring

power out
pipes leaking
flickering
of the candle

we were always traveling
yet we love to come home
like cats
crying to come in
wet with september rain

scent of eucalyptus
janis joplin coming
across the radio waves
the dj cuts in to announce
terrorists, hostages, plane crashes
it is 7am and
i am sitting beside my cat
drinking coffee
grateful for my
simple life

i went to
st. john the divine church
in nyc
to see the huge crystal
and to see some elephants
get blessed
candles burned down

watching the dance
of the dead
as I drink
my manhattan
cremation next

6 o'clock news
3 beheaded men
& a beer commercial

a beautiful woman
long smooth legs
steps out
of a 2000 mazda
miata
on the edge
of a manhattan
street
and in the sky
the twin towers
come down
in flames

today
my life feels
like a
dream sequence
in a
david lynch
movie

nyc
today
you are
as dark as
a van gogh
crow

9/11

you jumped
from the twins
holding hands

girlfriend leaves
cat dies—
the towers fall

can't sleep
3 a.m.
i hear
a fire engine horn
a black
cat meowing
on this cool
september
morning

he read rilke
outside st. john
the divine cathedral
beside a gargoyle

i danced with demons
shirley temple's small bones

in bed
reading zen
by a fading
candle

a gentle good night
to you dylan
sipping in the white horse tavern
fern hill
coming back to you

life is
black-stemmed goblets
and your thighs
by the fire
then in comes
the trojan
horse

in the stalled greyhound
a girl
with a red balloon

magic

reading tarot cards
my cat stretched out on table
clawing the death card

pouring rain
everything is cancelled
but sipping tea
and watching
the twilight zone

we sleep with
rabbit's feet
and horseshoes
to protect ourselves
against the packs
of black cats
who would slink
on the edges
of our dreams

sunday at st. mark's place

intellectuals strolling
in the sun
i gobble my sandwich
genoa salami
provolone cheese
and lunch poems

oh the humanity

upstate med
six floors
367 televisions on
the same blaring story

muzak in the lobby
and then the two boeings in the twins

beautiful september morning
brooks brothers suits
briefcases
the last time

are the pilots
now enjoying
their 72 houri

smell of ground zero
dust rising from bulldozers
t-shirts
black crow
on black steel

a man kept waving
a white shirt
from one of the floors
then jumped

bodies thumping
on the marriot inn

in the heaps of rubble
firemen's beepers
droning

cortland street
chambers street
church street
closed today

i believe in art
photography love
and poetry
it's hard for me

why did it happen
no answers
in my cups
of coors lite

some people mumbling
praying
about staying up
for monday nite football
and being late for work

the floors plunged
one after another
like dominos

empty stretchers line the halls
no burn victims will arrive

two columns of light
is all that remains

i search for you
like cats seek shade
from the hot noon sun

snow on tombstones
cathedral bells ring

1998 nyc

licking lemon ice
in the shade of the twin towers

sunday
starbucks coffee
new york times
art section
& walking along the hudson
with you

the voice of muddy waters
black cats at night

in darkness
i see a small candle
burning
i smell incense burning
i drink my wine
all alone

lavender sky
where the
twin towers
used
to
be

some days
are worse
than others
new york times newspapers
piled in the corner

terrorist car bomb
near the lion king
at times square

ash wednesday
the twin towers
are down

van gogh's shoes
rivers' camels
twin towers crumbling
dekooning's yellow slash
your naked thighs
always

gothic cathedral
13 sheep
24 hungry ghosts
another sleepless night

if you want
to get depressed

1. listen to the music of tom waits
2. watch documentaries about 9/11
3. fall in love with someone
   who doesn't love you back
4.

it's the nyc
skyscrapers
against the moon
and i'm in
attendance

the met

walking through
the metropolitan art museum
portraits
oranges
knives
watermelons
fish
a woman in a ditch
a medieval tapestry
with an unraveled stitch
thank god they didn't destroy this

power out
pipes leaking
flickering
of the candle

you were once as happy
as a bottle of wine
with a 1913 vintage
then in came
the man with the scythe

i am sick of watching
terrorists every night
on cnn
but there's
nothing else on

wrong time zone again

bought some jeans
today
translated three poems
drank some wine
and passed out on the sofa
with my cat
leaving all the clocks
behind

9/11

call in sick
stay in bed
all day reading
bukowski

tics
as the psychic
turns over
death

a friend of mine
from cantor fitzgerald
just died
i'm sitting here
listening to jane's addiction
drinking merlot

hot rum
snow
falling slowly
outside henrietta
hudson's windows
on the sidewalks
of ny

i pour myself
a glass of wine
and get too close
to the fire

"to get
to brooklyn
from manhattan
we have
to go under
the east
river" she said
"do you mind?"

things i love to do in nyc—
modern art museum
metropolitan art museum
yankees game
fucking you in central park

what a time
it was
broadway
boogie woogie
at the guggenheim

i'm going to see
el greco's
dried
fish

in my dreams
i wander
through dekooning paintings
wearing a yankees uniform

metropolitan art museum

i curl up
in front of renoir's
sleeping girl with a cat
and sleep

i think andy was lonely
with his factory
full of people

1960's telephone

whenever it
rings i

want to pull
it out of the wall

paint it
with stars and moons

and mail it to
the whitney art museum
20th century art exhibit

to be placed
between the hoover vacuum
and the lava lamps

nyc nightscape
out the window
of the bus
she loses
her jerry garcia
scarf

"frank"

naked
staring out
of canvases
at the modern art museum

used bookstore in brooklyn

a black cat
dreaming
beside a first edition
of
apollinaire

riding the D
to the
brooklyn museum
to see
basquait
who used to
graffiti
these trains

at my bedroom window
a balloon named felix
floats by

at the neue gallery
matare's *lurking cat*
catches my eye
i too would have been
degenerate
to the nazis

at the metropolitan art museum

there you were
bored as always
finding me transfixed
on a painting by redon
i was hopelessly in love
with you
like chagall
obsessed with bella
everything seemed
to be flying
in the air

we drove
in the east village
in your open mg
like two gurgling
draft beer spouts

egyptian cobra
descendant of the asp
that killed cleo
slithers away
from the bronx zoo

i never go
to nyc
without
lunch poems

could be a painter

art addicted
had to see
pissaro at the louvre
michelangelo at the gallerie di palazzo
dekooning at the modern
nylons hang over
the headboard
naked she puts up the blinds
looks out at
the new york city moon

new york city
    (after trakl)

toward night we hear the howls of cats
two black tails sticking out of garbage cans,
the green oak rustles,
you and i walk into an outdoor café
clams and wine taste great,
great: to stagger drunk into the streets.
voices, horses hoofs echo through
    the maple branches
love softens your face

Printed in the United States
By Bookmasters